A BOOK OF SEASONS

A Random House PICTUREBACK®

ALICE AND MARTIN PROVENSEN

A Book of

This title was originally catalogued by the Library of Congress as follows: Provensen, Alice. A book of seasons / Alice and Martin Provensen. New York: Random House, ©
1976. [32]p.: col. ill.; 21 cm. (A Random House Pictureback) SUMMARY: An easy-to-read description of the continuously changing seasons. 1. Seasons–Juvenile literature.
[1. Seasons] I. Provensen, Martin, joint author. II. Title. QB631.P76 500.9 75-36470 ISBN:0-394-83642-1 (B.C.); 0-394-83242-6 (trade); 0-394-93242-0 (lib. bdg.).

21 22 23 24 25 26 27 28 29 30 31   4 5 6 7 8 9 0

SEASONS

RANDOM HOUSE NEW YORK

Winter is here. Put on your boots. Find your mittens.
You can build a snowman.

Winter is the cold season of the year. It's a time
for snow shovels and warm woolen scarfs.

You can ride downhill on sleds when snow is on the ground.
But look! . . .What is happening?

The snow is melting. A bright purple flower is poking through the snow.

The days are longer.
The sap is running in the maple trees.

It's maple-syrup time.
It's the first day of spring.

Spring can be rainy.

Or spring can be sunny.

Spring is a breezy, blossomy season.

Everything is fresh and sweet and clean.

Summer follows spring.
The days grow longer and the nights are warm.

Take off your shoes.
Summer is the time to go barefoot.

Now you can be out of doors all day long.

It's fun to lie in the green grass and look at the sky.

In summer you can work in the garden.
You can plant a flower or watch a butterfly.

You can eat a green bean.
But summer doesn't last long.

The days begin to grow shorter and cooler.
The leaves turn red and orange and gold.

Put on your jacket and take a walk.
The first day of fall is here.

Now the leaves are brown and falling down.
It's fun to rake them up.

You can hide in a pile of leaves.
But not for long. Someone is sure to find you!

The days are colder now. It's time to cut firewood.

Fires are cozy on cold winter nights.

Suddenly one day the snow begins to fall.
Put on your hats! Don't forget your mittens!

Where are your boots?
It's the first day of winter again.

Once more it's the season for skates and sleds.
A whole year has passed.

A year is the time between one birthday and the next.
You can have a skating party if your birthday is in winter.

But look what is happening. The ice on the pond is breaking up.

The snow is melting. There's a little green leaf on the tree.

Spring is here again. Spring is the earth's birthday.
It comes again and again and again.